Eyewitness Accounts of the American Revolution

Personal Recollections
of
Captain Enoch Anderson

The New York Times & Arno Press

1 39 57

Reprint Edition 1971 by Arno Press Inc.

*

LC# 76-140851
ISBN 0-405-01221-7

*

Eyewitness Accounts of the American Revolution, Series III
ISBN for complete set: 0-405-01187-3

*

Manufactured in the United States of America

PERSONAL RECOLLECTIONS

OF

CAPTAIN ENOCH ANDERSON

1755-1837.

PAPERS OF THE HISTORICAL SOCIETY OF DELAWARE.

XVI.

PERSONAL RECOLLECTIONS

OF

CAPTAIN ENOCH ANDERSON,

AN OFFICER OF THE

DELAWARE REGIMENTS IN THE REVOLUTIONARY WAR.

WITH NOTES BY

HENRY HOBART BELLAS, LL.B.,

CAPTAIN U. S. ARMY,

Secretary Delaware State Society of the Cincinnati; Honorary Member Delaware and
New Hampshire Historical Societies; Member Pennsylvania Historical Society,
American Numismatic and Archæological Society of New York, etc.

THE HISTORICAL SOCIETY OF DELAWARE,
WILMINGTON.
1896.

PRESS OF J. B. LIPPINCOTT COMPANY, PHILADELPHIA.

PREFACE.

CAPTAIN ENOCH ANDERSON, the eldest son of William and Elizabeth (Inslee) Anderson, and the writer of the following recollections, was an officer in both Colonels Haslet and Hall's Delaware Regiments during the Revolution, and, as his letters show, was a faithful soldier and patriot. Though born in Pennsylvania, he served in the Delaware regiments, and after the war married and for several years resided near Newport, New Castle County, in this State. He removed, with his family, about 1787, to Cumberland County, and afterwards to Waterford, Juniata County, Pennsylvania, where he died. The record in his family Bible states that " he had a paralectic stroke on the morning of the thirteenth of April, 1824, and died on the twenty-first of April, in his seventieth year, and is buried in the grave yard of the meeting house near McCulloch's Mills, Juniata County, Pennsylvania." His wife, Eleanor McCalmont, lies buried with him.

Alexander Anderson, his nephew, and to whom he addressed these letters, was the second son of Major Joseph Anderson and his wife, Patience Outlaw (daughter of Colonel Alexander Outlaw, of Tennessee). Alexander Anderson was born in Jefferson County, East Tennessee, November 10, 1794, and died in Knoxville, Tennessee, May 23, 1869. He was elected United States senator from that

State in 1840, and was afterwards a legislator and judge of the Supreme Court of California. He also assisted in framing the constitution of the latter-named State. His only surviving son, General David Deaderick Anderson, a prominent lawyer of Knoxville, Tennessee, and for eight years attorney-general of Tennessee, now represents Major Joseph Anderson in the Delaware Cincinnati, while James Galbraith Anderson, of Pittsburg, Pennsylvania, the grandson of Captain Enoch Anderson, and the possessor of the originals of these letters, is the eldest lineal representative of the latter in the same Society.

It is hoped the information contained in this record, imperfect though it may seem, will be of value to the history of the State of Delaware in the Revolutionary period.

H. H. BELLAS.

OCTOBER 1, 1896.

LETTERS OF CAPTAIN ENOCH ANDERSON.

NUMBER ONE.

WATERFORD, PA., April 19, 1819.

DEAR NEPHEW:

Your letter is received. Agreeable I am to thank you for your attentions to my poor boy, my son Thomas.*   He speaks highly of you and indeed of all his relations.   I have now but little command of pen, though you wish me to give you a sketch of my military life in the Revolutionary War.   That is, to fight battles over again on paper.   Many of the scenes of those times are still fresh in my memory, but you must give me time.   I write but pot-hooks and hangers now,—can you read them?   Sometimes I can hardly read my own writing.   The frequent attacks of rheumatism have done this.   Yet God blesses me with high bodily health; yes, I am thankful to say, as much as when I was a young man.

You are to forgive me all egotisms, for no person speaking of himself but is more or less an egotist.   I shall speak the truth to the best of my knowledge, but the lapse of time has erased many things from my memory.

I was born at Newton,† Bucks County, Pennsylvania, on the 1st of May, 1754, about twenty-eight miles north-

---

* Thomas Fabius Anderson, sixth son of Captain Enoch Anderson, was born July 12, 1793, in Toboyne Township, Cumberland County, Pennsylvania, and died (unmarried) at Washington City, D. C., July 28, 1864.

† Now written *Newtown.*

east from Philadelphia. Your father * was born at the village of Whitemarsh, twelve miles north of Philadelphia; at that time, Philadelphia county. Your father is about one year and six months younger than I am.

Myself and brothers had in one respect a Roman education. The Roman youth were all taught athletic exercises to harden and invigorate the body and our father † encouraged these things,—but I believe we were all naturally inclined to such sports and pastimes. I was brought up to hardihood,—I was never idle but when I was sleeping,

---

* Major Joseph Anderson, who, according to another family record, was born 1757 instead of 1755. He served in the New Jersey Continental line (First and Third Regiments) through the Revolution, and was afterwards a resident of Delaware till appointed by President Washington United States judge of the territory south of the Ohio River. He assisted in framing the Constitution of Tennessee, was United States senator from that State from 1797 to 1815, and acted as president *pro tempore* of the Senate; was also first comptroller of the United States Treasury from 1815 till his death, in Washington City, D. C., April 17, 1837. He was an original member of the Delaware State Society of the Cincinnati, with Captain Enoch Anderson and two other of his brothers,—Thomas, a lieutenant in the Delaware regiment, and William, an ensign in the New Jersey line. (See History Delaware State Society of the Cincinnati, by Captain H. H. Bellas, U.S.A.; Papers of Historical Society of Delaware, No. XIII, pp. 54–55. Wilmington, Delaware, 1895.)

† William Anderson was a distinguished citizen of Philadelphia County, Pennsylvania. His character was so marked for honor, probity, and amiability that it is related of him that he elicited the observation of a friend who met him on the streets of Philadelphia, "You are the man upon whom a woe is pronounced. Woe to him of whom every one speaks well!" He died at an early period of the Revolution, leaving a widow, Elizabeth Inslee, by whom he had thirteen children; six sons and four daughters surviving. Five of these sons took an active part in the war.

reading or writing. God gave me a robust constitution, fitted to bear hardships and privations.

I was appointed a second lieutenant in the First company in the Delaware Regiment,—(but one Regiment in the State),—in August or September, 1775. I was about nineteen years of age. I had now taken on myself the character of a soldier, with a determined mind to rough the storms of life and those of war. I was now sent on the recruiting business and the company was soon raised, as my mind was now intent on this thing. I had got some rudiments of tacticks in the militia from an old British deserter. We had no arms but were busy throughout the winter of '75 and '6, in training our men as well as we could without arms.

In April '76, we were ordered from Wilmington (our quarters) to Dover, fifty miles down the Bay of Delaware. Here the whole Regiment was completed in May '76, but had yet no arms. An old British Captain, Thomas Holland, left the British army from principle and joined us. He was our Adjutant, an excellent disciplinarian and brought on the Regiment fast.

The Tories in the lower county (Sussex), bordering on the Bay of Delaware, began to make some hostile movements. Arms were now got for about two hundred of our Regiment. In this command I went under the command of our Major,—Macdonough,*—(the father of Commodore

---

* Thomas Macdonough (1747–1795) was the eldest son of James Macdonough, of the Trappe, New Castle County, Delaware. His services as Major of Colonel John Haslet's regiment of Delaware State troops in the early years of the Revolution are already well-known. (See Memoir of Commodore Thomas Macdonough, by Lewis C. Vandegrift, Esq.; Papers of His-

Macdonough), to Lewistown * at the mouth of the Delaware and near the light-house. Here we were in the land of Tories—the British men-of-war lying in the bay opposite to us,—not more than one mile,—and in the interior, surrounded by these Tories. Our situation was indeed perilous. There were some good Whigs in the town, but there were also Tories. Our worthy Major kept a sharp lookout;—it became us all to be vigilant and we were so, and for young soldiers I think we done our duty.

By this time, from the attentions of our Adjutant—Holland—to me and from his tuition, I was considered a tolerable disciplinarian. This worthy man (Holland), became partial to me,—lived with me,—let me into his whole history, and such a history! So variegated with the ups and downs of Life!—but I shall have occasion to mention him again in this narration.

I was now for the first time in my life sent on a command to a post of danger. Eight miles below the light-house is a bending of the sea-shore and mariners coming in would take it for the Bay of Delaware and many ships have thus been lost there. The British at this time were taking our vessels every day and it was for this reason called the False Capes. I was sent there to protect any of our shipping and mariners that might be driven on this false cape. It is eight miles from Lewistown. I had thirty men—all young fellows—with me. We travelled through rich black land

torical Society of Delaware, No. XII. Wilmington, Delaware, 1895.) His great-grandson, Rodney Macdonough, is now his eldest lineal male representative in the Delaware State Cincinnati.

* Now always written *Lewes*.

and came to the place of our destination and a beautiful spot it was. I made up my quarters at Captain Hazzard's,* —a militia captain and a Whig. Here then I was placed at the post of danger to guard and defend, &c., but nothing happened and no vessels were driven on shore. Oysters and fish were plenty. I was stationed there for two weeks and then me and my boys returned to Lewis Town.

All was now peace and quietness,—I hated to be idle,— my father and family had moved to New Castle and I wanted to see them. I had been a waterman,—a fine large boat lay on the sea-shore, wafted there from some of the vessels the British had taken from us, for they would often scuttle them and send them adrift. It is about one hundred miles from New Castle to Lewis Town. My Captain permitted me to go with two soldiers, and in two and a-half days I was at New Castle in the bosom of my family. I stayed here and among my acquaintances for about a week. My father gave me a horse, saddle and bridle when I left.

I went to Dover. Here all was confusion. The Tories had risen in Sussex, it was said,—our troops were surrounded in Lewistown and would be all cut off. That

---

* Captain Cord Hazzard was the eldest son of Joseph and grandson of Cord Hazzard, of Stretcher's Island, Broadkill Creek, Sussex County, Delaware, who settled in this State in 1700. Captain Hazzard was born April 28, 1750, and died March 13, 1831. He served in Colonels Haslet and Hall's regiments until March, 1778, when (on the authority of Governor Caleb P. Bennett, his companion in arms) " he resigned his commission, owing to the loss of his hearing by the bursting of a shell during the attack by the British on Mud Island, below Philadelphia, in November, 1777." (See History of Delaware Cincinnati, pp. 73, 77.) His representatives are still residing in Sussex County, Delaware.

to-morrow a regiment of Tories would be at Dover to de-stroy the town. I was up at daylight when their militia infantry was paraded. I went to them. "Come," said I, "give me a gun, powder and ball,—I will be a private in your company." These things were got for me with thank-fulness and here we stood on parade,—about forty of us,—till nine o'clock. No enemy appeared and I was now deter-mined to push for Lewistown, fifty miles ahead, with the country lined with Tories. My friends were much opposed to my going, but I was determined and on I went. This was still in May, '76.

I had not ridden more than two miles till I was met by a whole Regiment of Tories going to Dover. I was in regi-mentals and they knew to where I belonged, yet so it was they let me pass peaceably on. Some miles further on, I came to a tavern full of Tories. Strange to say they also let me pass, but not more than a quarter of a mile in ad-vance of the tavern, I was met by about thirty Tories all armed. "Here," said they, "is one of d——d Haslet's men,"—(Haslet* was the name of our Colonel, who was very obnoxious to them being a firm friend to his country.) —"You're a d——d rebel, we have got you now and will take care of you."

I thought of the "Roebuck" man-of-war,—I was not far from the Delaware and was fearful I was to take up lodgings on board of the British man-of-war.

---

* Colonel John Haslet, who fell, a martyr to his country, at Princeton, January 3, 1777. The history of his life is part of that of the State of Delaware.

"Light down this minute, you d——d rebel," was my next invitation, and twenty guns were presented. I got off my horse,—I was in a bad situation and I wished I had stayed at Dover. They pulled off my saddle-bags and strewed the ground with their contents. The best way I thought was to put a good grace on a bad matter, for I was indeed in a woeful situation,—in a perilous situation by my own imprudence. I often thought of Dover where I might have been safe, and then of the "Roebuck" where I was to be a prisoner shortly.

I now began to tell them some merry stories and among other things I told them if they would behave themselves quietly and decently and not be in the habit of stopping people on the road and ransacking their baggage,—as they had done mine,—I would try to make their peace with our Major. They swore I was a d——d impudent fellow, but a jolly one, then they gathered up all my things, put on my saddle-bags again and let me go.

This night I had a quiet night's rest and I was on my way betimes the next morning about ten o'clock. I found the country in a bustle. I came to a tavern about eight miles from my destination (Lewistown). At this tavern there was a great gathering of the people and a great stir among them. I thought to myself, "no good unto me," but I must stop as my horse must be fed. A trough was at the door and my horse was fed. These fellows eyed me, —I eyed them in return, and again I thought of the "Roebuck." They were so keen upon me, I thought they would lay hold of me. At this moment I called for a pint of rum which was set on the table and I paid my bill.

"Come my jolly fellows," says I, "let us take a joram."
I drank a little and whilst they were busy about the bottle,
I slipped out and onto my horse and was gone! They
missed me at once and hallooed "come back you d——d
rebel;—you d——d Haslet's man!" But I was out of
their reach and in Lewistown before night.

"No battles yet," you say;—but as I go on, they will
come. Write on sight of this. All our loves to you all.

Your uncle with affection.

Enoch Anderson *

ALEX^R. ANDERSON, ESQ^R.

---

* This signature is a *fac-simile* of that on a petition of the officers of the
Delaware Regiment to the General Assembly of the State, dated April 18,
1776, requesting the appointment of John Corse to a lieutenancy in the
regiment.

Unfortunately no portrait of Captain Anderson is known, or believed, to
exist.

NUMBER TWO.

My last ended when I had run the gauntlet, escaped the Tories and arrived safe at Lewistown. I was congratulated on my safe arrival, for had I been but one day later I must have fallen a prisoner in the hands of the Tories. All was alarm at our garrison; the Whig militia and many officers had come in and put themselves under the protection of our little Army, and to give what aid they could, but our whole force did not amount to more than three hundred men. We had one "long Tom," which was given in to the charge of a Major Fisher,* a spirited militia officer, and some of his select companions.

The alarm increased. I think it was the third day after my arrival that we were surrounded by about fifteen hundred Tories. A Council of safety was formed of fifteen members of the Whig militia officers by the desire of our Major. The Major came to me and took me with him to this council of safety;—General Dagworthy† was the chairman.

---

* A fund, it is understood, is now (1896) being raised to erect a monument in memory of Major Henry Fisher, who was a Delaware pilot and did good service in the Revolution. He is buried at Lewes, and deserves such proposed tribute to his memory.

† For an account of the life and services of Brigadier-General John Dagworthy in the Colonial and Revolutionary Wars, see "Memoir of General Dagworthy," by George W. Marshall, M.D. (Papers of Historical Society of Delaware, No. X, Wilmington, Delaware, 1895.)

"This," says our Major, "is the young man I have recommended to your notice." "Why," says the Chairman, "this is but a beardless boy." "No matter," said the Major, "I think him fitted to the office you may appoint him." The Chairman rose up and addressed me then, as near as I can remember, in the following manner, viz:

"You must be well informed of our dangerous situation. Here are five British men-of-war in the Bay right opposite us,—not more than a mile off,—and we are surrounded by about fifteen hundred Tories three miles off, who, we are credibly informed, keep up a regular correspondence with the British fleet in the Bay. We therefore, young man, do constitute and appoint you Adjutant General *pro tem.*, under the command of the Commander-in-chief, Major Macdonough. The Tories, (said he,) are mostly armed with guns, and those that have not guns have pitch-forks and down to clubs. Now, young man, a great responsibility is thrown on your shoulders. Be careful,—be vigilant; —under Major Macdonough all your orders are to be obeyed."

I told the council I wished to decline the honour of this high office,—I was not fitted for it;—but the Major insisted upon it and the Council pressed it. Now I knew no more about the duties of an Adjutant General than the man in the Moon. I had but in a manner learned the first rudiments of tacticks, and my friend Holland was not here from whom I could have got instruction;—he was at Wilmington with the other part of the Regiment, more than a hundred miles off, at near the north end of the State.

I made my bow to the Council,—thanked them for the honour they had done me, and said, that with my small abilities, I should use every exertion in my power. The Major and me left the Council-room. I now consulted him what was best to be done. " I leave it all to you," said he.

In the evening I had our whole force paraded,—my authority was previously made known. I gave special orders for every man to lay on his arms this night and to be ready to turn out at a minute's notice. I now took thirty men from the right and at dark planted them as sentinels round the town at one hundred yards distance. I gave them the watch-word or countersign,—"*Washington*,"—and instructed them that if any person cannot give you this word, to take him prisoner—and if he tries to make his escape, to fire at him and bring him to. That the first sentinel on the right shall cry " all's well!" every half-hour, and if not well, to give the alarm. This was to go its rounds throughout thirty sentinels. That in two hours, I would bring thirty more to relieve them.

I came to my quarters,—but not to sit down ;—no, my clothes were not off all this night nor did I sleep a wink. My boys, my sentinels, instead of crying " all's well" each half-hour, began to cry it every ten minutes, and at last constantly on, which made a constant bellowing and a great noise. It was thought in town the Tories were coming. I went out with thirty new men to relieve the former sentinels and again gave special orders to cry " all's well" every half-hour, but these were worse than the others! Suffice it to say, that throughout the whole night this bawling of " all's well" was kept up by these young soldiers.

It was the same thing the next night. Now, contrary to all expectation, this noise had a good effect. The Tories had conceived we were rejoicing from aid we must have got from above and which had come down the Bay to our assistance, so that in a few days they were willing to make peace and to bury the tomahawk. They were to remain neutral and to keep the peace.

And now I resigned my great appointment of Adjutant General with great satisfaction,—having held it for six days and nights;—during which time I never had my clothes off and lost much rest.

All was now peace and quietness,—our Major went by land to Wilmington and the command devolved on our Captain,—Stidham,* a worthy man,—being the oldest Captain in the Regiment. General Washington hearing of our dangerous situation,—being planted between two fires, the British on one side and the Tories on the other,—ordered Colonel Miles' Regiment of Riflemen of four hundred men to our assistance. They came after our peace with the Tories and found all quietness; staid a few days and returned to headquarters at New York. Our Captain (Stidham) was then ordered to join the other part of the Regiment at Wilmington. This was in June, '76.

There was a large shallop and oyster-boat at Lewistown, and as he preferred a water conveyance to travelling by land to Wilmington, the baggage was put on board the shallop,

---

* Captain Joseph Stidham's name appears on the roll of officers of Colonel Haslet's regiment of Delaware State troops in Continental service, with date of commission, as such, of January 13, 1776. (See History of Delaware State Cincinnati, p. 73.)

and he ordered me to take fifteen men and go aboard of the oyster-boat. Now this boat was a crazed thing,—it had no hatches and was leaky. I represented this thing to Captain Stidham, but he said the weather was fine and there was no danger. (I had been a waterman and he knew it.)

We set off in the evening without a pilot. Among my little crew I chose two soldiers, that had been seamen, to give aid, &c. We had not got more than five miles from Lewis Town, when the heavens were overcast with clouds and I expected a storm. It came on from the north-east with violence. The shallop was in rear of me about half-a-mile and we were about a mile, I thought, from the Delaware shore. The night was on us,—it grew very dark,—the storm increased, but we could still see the light of the light-house. I asked my two sailors was it not best to cast out our anchor, and they thought it would be. It was cast out,—we happened on good anchorage grounds. The storm increased,—from the rain and mist we had now lost sight of the light-house, and it was thought we were dragging out to sea. The storm still increased and our crazy boat, I was afraid, would go to the bottom. The waves run very high and would dash over us from bow to stern, so that we were filling with water very fast.

The whole crew had now given themselves up to a hopeless condition,—that they would all be lost, &c. Our boat was knocked about in a horrid manner, no one being able to stand on the deck. These two sailors began to make a noise,—saying we were all lost and prayed lustily. This set the others going, and what with the noise of the whistling

2

of the wind, the driving of the waves, and the darkness of the night,—things looked gloomy indeed.

I now ordered one of the sailors to go forward and feel our cable,—to know whether we dragged or not,—but he would not stir a foot, saying we were all lost,—that out at sea he never was in such a storm before. I spoke to others —but not one man would go forward to see to our anchor, though the boat had now three feet of water in the hold. I then stripped off all my clothes, but my shirt and breeches, and crept along to the bow. Here I felt the cable and found it did *not* drag. I gave out the good word and it revived some, but my two sailors still cried out there was no hope; —they were linked together, holding fast of the rails of the quarter-deck. We had two camp-kettles on board and I now forced some soldiers into the hold to throw out the water. They threw some out but said it increased on them. I then proposed to run the vessel on shore, but to this they all disagreed, saying " let us all take our lots together!"

Never, I thought, was I in such danger in my life. My men were stupid with very fear,—my two sailors praying made a great noise,—indeed, that discouraged the others. I had very serious thoughts myself and looked upwards in silent prayer.

In this night of our misery, I thought of a canteen of rum I had on board. I gave them a joram and got them again into the hold to throw out the water. I offered to join them myself, but they would not let me. Rum never did more good, they threw out the water rapidly,—daybreak came,— the wind abated,—we saw the shallop a half-a-mile in our rear, and we all returned to Lewis Town.

Captain Stidham now got a pilot and the next day we set sail,—the whole force on board the shallop,—with the wind fair and the weather good. In less than forty hours we were at Wilmington and joined our comrades.

Affectionately Your Uncle,

ENOCH ANDERSON.

ALEXANDER ANDERSON, EsqR.

April 29, 1819.

NUMBER THREE.

MY last brought us to Wilmington. In a few days afterwards, the fourth of July came on, and our Regiment marched to New Castle, the county-town of New Castle County (Delaware). We took out of the Court-House all the insignias of Monarchy,—all the baubles of Royalty, and made a pile of them before the Court-House,—set fire to them and burnt them to ashes. This was our first jubilee on the fourth of July, '76, and a merry day we made of it. We returned to Wilmington in the evening, and in a few days after, we took up our line of march for headquarters.

The first day we came to Philadelphia and took up our cantonment in the Barracks north of the city. Here our Regiment was completely armed and fully equipped for war, —all in regimentals,—five hundred, rank and file. We proceeded on to our place of destination—headquarters,—at New York,—and in a few days we arrived there.

Here was a new order of things,—new to us. Tents were given out to us and we encamped in them, about a mile north of the city. A large fleet of men-of-war and transports belonging to the enemy, lay in the harbour, about two miles below the city. They had taken possession of Staten Island but had not yet landed on Long Island, but it was expected every day that they would do so.

After some days our Regiment, with others, was ordered on Long Island. Here were many fortifications. In August, through a night, the enemy landed a large body, and the alarm-gun was fired at three o'clock in the morning.

THE BATTLE OF LONG ISLAND.

A little before day, as we marched towards the enemy, two miles from our camp we saw them. A little after daylight our Regiment and Colonel Smallwood's Regiment from Maryland, in front of the enemy took possession of a high commanding ground,—our right to the harbour. Cannonading now began in both armies. Captain Stidham was ordered out with his company to feel his way nearer to the British and skirmish. We soon fell in with a solid body of them. It appeared their aim was to surround us,—we gave them a fair fire,—every man levelled well. I saw one man tumble from his horse,—never did I take better aim at a bird, —yet I know not that I killed any or touched any. The fire was returned and they killed two of our men dead,— none wounded. It became proper for us to retreat and we retreated about four hundred yards and were joined by Colonel Atlee's Regiment, commanded by Lieutenant-Colonel Parry.*

The British pressed hard upon us with far superior numbers and here began our part of the battle in our part of the army. Colonel Parry was killed. I was wounded,—a bullet

---

* Written Purey in the manuscript, evidently an error. Lieutenant-Colonel Caleb Parry commanded Colonel Samuel J. Atlee's musketry battalion in the battle on Long Island, the latter-named officer having been captured. For account of the services of these officers and of the battle of Long Island, see Pennsylvania State Archives, 2d series, vol. x, pp. 193–253.

struck me on the chin and run down into my neck. Many fell, many were wounded. About three o'clock in the afternoon a retreat was ordered. We crossed over a mill-dam on a foot-bridge. The Regiment began to move in a few minutes after we had got over the bridge, and waded through the mill-dam,—neck-deep,—far below the foot-bridge. For ten minutes after I had crossed the foot-bridge with our company, our Regiment was surrounded and no escape remained for them but for to wade the mill-dam. Some men were lost.

Colonel Smallwood's Regiment took another course,— they were surrounded but they fought hard. They lost about two hundred men, the rest got in. A hard day this, for us poor Yankees! Superior discipline and numbers had overcome us. A gloomy time it was, but we solaced ourselves that at another time we should do better.

Some days after this a retreat was ordered in the night. Our Regiment was the last that left our lines. We set off at daybreak,—a thick fog arose ;—it was the pillar of a cloud to our enemies and favorable to us. Under it we all got off the Island, save a few individuals.

We now moved to the north end of York Island,—here we threw up some intrenchments. General Washington relinquished the city of New York and came himself to the north end of the Island, and with him all our little army.

We were encamped near the walls of Fort Washington. Many small conflicts took place between our out-parties and the British. In one of these, Colonel Reed, * one of Gen-

---

* General Joseph Reed (1741–1785) served with the American army till the close of 1777, when he was elected to Congress, and the following year governor of Pennsylvania. Though he was undoubtedly patriotic, and always

eral Washington's aids (afterwards Governor of Pennsylvania),—rode towards the line. He met a New England sergeant running off and the Colonel stopped him to turn him back. He up with his gun to fire at the Colonel, but his gun burnt priming. He was taken prisoner, tried by a court-martial and condemned to be shot.

"Why," you would ask, "am I thus particular, on this trifling occurrence?" I answer—"Stop, till I tell you."

The day of execution came,—a fine day,—and our whole army was drawn up in a circle. The lot fell on the Delaware Regiment to find an officer and men to shoot this man. Major Macdonough came to me and said, "You must go with some soldiers and do this thing." I chose out twenty soldiers and went on the hateful business. A small parapet was thrown up near the edge of the circle of the army. I consulted my friend Holland on the occasion.

I drew near to the fatal spot;—the prisoner was kneeling in front of the parapet, with a cap over his eyes. We came within twenty feet of him,—his every nerve was creeping, and in much agony he groaned. I groaned, my soldiers groaned, —we all groaned. I would rather have been in a battle. After he was worked up to a high degree for an example to the army, perhaps, a minister mounted the parapet and cried "a pardon, a pardon!" The poor condemned thing tried to look upward, but could not,—he was bound in fetters. He cried out, "oh! Lord God, oh! I am not to be shot—oh! oh!"

---

retained the confidence and esteem of Washington, General Reed was a strong partisan, and some of his acts as governor of the State of Pennsylvania have been the subject of bitter controversy.

Such are the feelings of sympathy, that the tears of joy run down my cheeks. I was not above my poor boys, each also shed their tears. Gloomy as was the morning, the evening turned out crowned with pleasure. This man I was afterwards informed went to General Washington and begged he might not be turned out of the army, to be sent home with disgrace upon his head, but be allowed to serve as a private soldier, that he might retrieve his character. It was granted, and I understood that he behaved well afterwards.

Our Regiment was encamped near the North River. The Island here from the North River to the East River is about a mile in width. A British man-of-war came up the North River and as it passed, they gave us some vollies of grape-shot among our tents, and some bombs. The grape-shot made holes in our tents, and some of the bombs broke in the air. One fell amidst our tents, but one of our boys ran and soon had pulled out the fuze. We had one man wounded.

We lay here some weeks. In October, General Howe sailed from New York with a fleet of transports and men-of-war and landed at Frog's (Throck's or Throgg's ?) Neck, —some miles above us. A council of war was held,—and we marched to the White Plains where we threw up intrenchments and expected the enemy. This country has many stone fences.

BATTLE OF WHITE PLAINS, OCTOBER 28, 1776.

About three thousand men—(the Delaware Regiment included)—were ordered to a hill, half a mile from our encampment, commanded by General McDougall. The whole force of the left wing of the British bore against us on the hill and a severe cannonading took place on both sides. Now began our firing with small arms on the hill and a hot fire was kept up for some time. Many lives were lost on both sides and many were wounded.

A soldier of our Regiment was mortally wounded in this battle. He fell to the ground ;—in falling, his gun fell from him. He picked it up,—turned on his face,— took aim at the British, who were advancing,—fired,—the gun fell from him,—he turned over on his back and expired. I forget his name.

We were ordered to retreat. We did so, in good order. When we got to camp, we found all our baggage, artillery, &c., were gone. We followed, and in the evening caught up with our army. This night we lay in the woods without tents or blankets. It was cold and we made a fire in the woods,—turned our feet to the fire and slept comfortably, although it snowed in the night.

We now moved to North Castle, but had no tents, no blankets. Buckwheat straw was plenty, however, which was a great comfort to us all. We were now under the command of General Lee. Orders were given to march up the North River and I was left with thirty men to pick up all stragglers.

E. ANDERSON.

ALEX^R. ANDERSON, ESQ.
     May 13, 1819.

NUMBER FOUR.

MY last (No. 3) ended where I was left in the rear to pick up all stragglers belonging to our army. My men and me searched, but found none. The army was now far ahead and we passed on to catch up. We had been but a few minutes on our march, when a man accosted us with " where are you going?" (He was about one hundred yards distance on horse-back.) " Come here," says I, " and I will tell you, and if you do not come, I will fire on you." He got into the bushes,—my men fired, but I believe he got off safe. We supposed him to be a spy.

We caught up with the army, and in a few days we were over the North River and into Jersey. General Washington had crossed the North River below us, and now commenced the memorable, the distressing retreat through Jersey of which you have, must have, read. We arrived at Brunswick, broken down and fatigued;—some without shoes, some had no shirts. This was the beginning of December, '76.

Colonel Haslet sent for me and told me I was appointed a Captain; the date of my commission being the third of December, 1776. It was soon known by the Regiment. The times of enlistments of almost the whole army were about expiring,—but gloomy as the times were, that very evening twenty-two men of our old Regiment and mostly of our old company, came to enlist with me for three years or during the war. Part of our Regiment was lodged in the Barracks and part in tents in front of the Barracks.

In the afternoon of the fifth of December, I think, the British appeared on the bank of the Raritan River. We were now under the command of Lord Stirling. He ordered his Brigade in front of the Barracks,—a severe cannonading took place on both sides, and several were killed and wounded on our side. Orders were now given for a retreat. It was near sundown. Our Regiment was in the rear. Colonel Haslet came to me and told me to take as many men as I thought proper, and go back and burn all the tents. "We have no wagons," said he, "to carry them off, and it is better to burn them than they should fall into the hands of the enemy." Then I went and burned them,— about one hundred tents.

When we saw them reduced to ashes, it was night and the army far ahead. We made a double quick-step and came up with the army about eight o'clock. We encamped in the woods, with no victuals, no tents, no blankets. The night was cold and we all suffered much, especially those who had no shoes.

The next day, we got to Princetown,* and here we had comfortable lodgings in the College. The whole army was now about twenty-five hundred men, and as their enlistments expired, they went off by hundreds. Our Regiment, although many of the men's enlistments were up, stuck to [*the army*].†

---

* Now written *Princeton*.

† All *italicized* words in brackets are insertions by the annotator, being either evident omissions by Captain Anderson, or considered as necessary to a clear understanding of the text.

The British were now in chase of us with twenty thousand men, within three miles of us. We continued on our retreat; —our Regiment in the rear, and I, with thirty men, in rear of the Regiment, and General Washington in my rear with pioneers,—tearing up bridges and cutting down trees, to impede the march of the enemy. I was to go no faster than General Washington and his pioneers.

It was dusk before we got to Trenton. Here we stayed all night. In the afternoon of the next day, we crossed the Delaware into Pennsylvania, and in two hours afterwards the British appeared on the opposite bank and cannonaded us; but we were in the woods and bushes and none were wounded that I heard of.

This was the crisis of American danger. This night we lay amongst the leaves without tents or blankets, laying down with our feet to the fire. It was very cold. We had meat, but no bread. We had nothing to cook with, but our ramrods, which we run through a piece of meat and roasted it over the fire, and to hungry soldiers it tasted sweet.

The next day we moved up the Delaware. In this way we lived, crouching among the bushes, till about the twelfth of December, '76, when I was sent for and some other officers of the Regiment, by Colonel Haslet. (The Colonel lived in a house.) " Here," said he, " is one hundred dollars for each of you Captains; the enlistments of the old Regiment are nearly out, and some have been out for some time. I shall stay here with the Army,"—(the other two field officers * were absent),—" go you to the State of Delaware,

---

* Lieutenant-Colonel Gunning Bedford and Major Thomas Macdonough.

recruit and raise your companies as soon as may be, and bring them on to camp." We set off,—four of us,—forthwith; others followed after us the next day, and a few days brought me to New Castle.

This closed the campaign of '76. These were called "the times that tried men's souls," and truly [*they were*] so. God spared me; for throughout all the scenes and sufferings of the campaign, I was not sick a day. I had read the History of Charles XII., King of Sweden, who had inured himself by degrees to the exposure of all weathers, so that he could lay down on the snow of Norway in mid-winter in sixty degrees of north latitude and take a nap! It was fun then to me. I now often thought of Charles the Twelfth.

CAMPAIGN OF 1777.

I begun the recruiting business. It went slowly on until General Washington had taken the Hessians at Trenton and defeated the British at Princetown; when, after this, it went on more briskly. Those I had enlisted at Brunswick joined me, and my company was complete early in the spring;—so was Captain Kirkwood's of our Regiment. We marched on to Philadelphia, and here we stayed some days to complete our companies in clothing, arms, &c. In a few days we were ready,—our two companies all in new regimentals, new arms and fully supplied with ammunition,—now fitted for war and to try a new campaign.

We got to our place of destination (Princetown), where General Putnam had the command. We found we were the only regular troops here, the others were militia;—perhaps in all not more than three hundred men. General Putnam now left us and General Sullivan took the command. General Washington lay at Middle Brook (Jersey), sixteen miles from Brunswick, the British headquarters. From Princetown to Brunswick was eighteen miles. We were all in a dangerous situation. Perhaps our whole force was not more than four thousand, and the British at Brunswick amounted to fifteen thousand. But such was the art of our old General that he made the enemy believe he had thousands, when he had not hundreds.

General Howe now marched his whole army towards General Washington's army and we were ordered to join our main army. This was in May when we joined General Washington. General Howe came forth in great force to Somerset Court-House, but finding he could not bring General Washington to action, he returned to Brunswick. About this time reinforcements had come on; the rest of our Regiment having joined us and others from other States. General Howe came out again to force General Washington to action, and this brought on the battle of Short Hills. Your father was in this battle.

General Howe now marched to Brunswick, to Amboy, to Staten Island and thence to New York. Philadelphia was his aim, but he found Jersey so full of enemies, he determined on another route. Sixteen thousand men, including cavalry, were put on board transports and they proceeded to sea. This was in June. The Maryland line and the Delaware Regiment were encamped near Morristown under the command of General Sullivan. The command of Jersey troops lay at Elizabethtown. We laid a plan to make a descent on Staten Island at this time.

We began our march at dark, marched twenty miles to the Sound, and crossed over to the Island. Here I was appointed to the command of seventy men from our Regiment as a flank guard, to keep at two or three hundred yards distance on the left from the main body. Captain Herron * of the Maryland line—with seventy men—on the van.

About sun-rise my line of march brought me near to a large brick house, on another part of the Sound. Here I found some of the British. But a few only of them turned out,—got round a hay-stack,—fired one gun and then run. I drew up my men on the pavement and entered the house. An old female was here, and no more. I soon found this was a colonel's quarters, with his officers. She told me I had come so quickly upon them, that they had run half-naked out of the house. I found the house full of lawful plunder. I went out to my soldiers and told them there was plenty of fair plunder inside. "Go in, all of you," I said, "I will stay here, but when you hear me beat the drum, come out in a moment." I waited a due time and then beat the drum. They came out,—each one had something.

As I was ready to march, Herron came with his party for plunder, and in the house he and all his soldiers went. He wanted me to wait, but I found the army was gone and I

---

* Should be *Heron.* Captain James Heron was an officer in Hazen's additional Continental regiment, which was brigaded with the Maryland and Delaware lines. He was taken prisoner on Staten Island, as stated, August 22, 1777, and resigned from the service in 1780. (See Heitman's Historical Register of Officers of Continental Army.)

told him I would not. At this moment a runner came to
tell me and Herron to come on directly,—that the enemy
had landed troops from Long Island and would waylay us
at the Red House. (I had already passed by this Red
House.) I hallooed to Herron, who was in the upper story
throwing out hats, &c., but he said he would not move until
he and his soldiers were loaded with plunder!

I marched on, and I had not gone three hundred yards
from the house when I was met by Colonel Stone at full
gallop. "Run, run," says he, "it's no disgrace." I passed
the Red House by a short cut through a meadow filled
with bushes,—my men in single file and leaving the Red
House to the right,—doubled my files and marched on with
a double quick step. I had not gone more than a quarter of
a mile, when a battle took place in my rear. This was
Herron marching by the Red House. He was attacked
here by the British,—had eighteen killed and wounded and
all the rest were taken prisoners,—plunder and all. I continued my march at a double quick time and came to the
place of crossing.

Here was great confusion,—no commander,—soldiers
running at their will, and not boats enough; there being
some unhappy error about the boats. I saw a boat coming
over and kept my eye on it, and as it came nearer the shore,
I came nearer to it. I kept my men in solid body and I
and my company entered the boat. We got safe over and
here I met your father. He had been on another part of
the island. Our Regiment had crossed long previous to me.

For want of boats, between two and three hundred men
fell into the hands of the British; for soon after we had got

over, a large body of the enemy appeared and surrounded our men [*left on the Island*] who surrendered. The Jersey troops got much spoil,—fair game. The Delaware Regiment got nothing, save what was taken by my company. One of the officers in my troops gave me a share of his spoils, but it was not much.

Now my good nephew, can you read these scratches of thy old uncle?

With affection,

ENOCH ANDERSON.

ALEX^R. ANDERSON, ESQ^R.
WATERFORD, May 20, 1819.

NUMBER FIVE.*

IN my last letter [*I ended with our getting back*] to the Jersey shore.

*   *   [*Original letter badly mutilated.*]   *   *

[*What with*] marching and countermarching, [*and often*] not knowing which [*way to go,*] . . . we continued in this

---

* The history of this period of the Revolution coincides with Captain Anderson's account. The movements of the American and British armies at this time are briefly related by an excellent authority (and may be here cited to elucidate the above imperfect narration) as follows : "Washington, as we have seen, was perplexed by the movements of Howe, being uncertain of his destination. As soon, however, as he was informed that the enemy's fleet was off the capes of the Chesapeake, he turned his attention in that direction. The detachments in New Jersey, whom General Sullivan had employed in unsuccessful enterprises against Staten Island, were recalled, and the whole army left Philadelphia for Wilmington. General Stephen with his division, with that of General Lincoln, . . . first proceeded to Chester; in which vicinity the militia of lower Pennsylvania and Delaware were gathering in large numbers, for the country was thoroughly aroused.

"The divisions of Stirling, Sullivan, and Greene, with Morgan's corps and Bland's regiment of horse, accompanied by Washington in person, left Philadelphia on the morning of the twenty-fourth of August, and encamped at Red Clay Creek, a few miles below Wilmington, the next day. The principal portion of the American cavalry were under the immediate command of Count Pulaski. General Nash, with Proctor's artillery, embarked in flat-boats upon the Delaware and proceeded to Chester, from whence he pressed forward to Wilmington. The whole effective force then present, and fit for duty, consisted of about eleven thousand men, including about eighteen hundred of Pennsylvania militia.

[*part of the country until the*] beginning of August. When the British [*transports*] had entered the Chesapeake Bay, [*we received orders*] to move to the Southward. Your [*father and I were together in those*] days,—we were in the neighborhood [*of our old home*]. Here in my old neighborhood, [*General Washington ordered*] intrenchments to be thrown

---

" Washington established his headquarters at Wilmington" (on the 31st, and, it is stated, on Quaker Hill, on West between Third and Fourth Streets, a site which should be marked), " and made immediate preparations to oppose the march of the enemy; he having been informed, by scouts, of their arrival at the Head of Elk. The Pennsylvania and Delaware Militia—the former under General Armstrong, the latter under General Rodney—were ordered to press forward to the Head of Elk and secure the stores deposited there. In this, however, they failed, the British army having already debarked, marched up as far as Iron Hill, and captured the stores. . . . The American forces took position on Red Clay Neck, about half way between Wilmington and Christiana, with the left on Christiana Creek, and their right extending towards Chad's ford on the Brandywine. . . . This position was eventually abandoned early on the morning of the 9th of September, for the more advantageous one finally assumed across the Brandywine, on the heights east of Chad's ford and commanding that passage of the stream. . . .

" Frequent skirmishes took place prior to the latter date between the American and British scouting parties, and on the third of September, a severe fight occurred at Pencander between the opposing forces. After the fight, the enemy burned Cooch's mills and the county records and buildings at Elkton. . . . On the eighth they moved forward by way of Newark and took post within four miles of the American army's right, whereupon Washington, believing it to be the design of Howe to turn his right, cut off his communication with Philadelphia and hem his army in between the British fleet and army, immediately fell back, as stated, across the Brandywine to a safe position." (See Lossing's Field Book of the Revolution, vol. ii. pp. 169–172, Edn. 1860; also address by Francis H. Hoffecker, Esq., before Historical Society of Delaware, Wilmington, Delaware, 1896, on " Delaware in the Revolution.")

up. . . . [*The British landed at the*] Head of Elk and took a circuitous route [*towards Wilmington*] and the Delaware. The army was [*encamped now on the*] Brandywine,—part of our army was [*drawn up at*] Chad's ford on the Brandywine and on the hills. The Delaware Regiment, by orders, encamped at Painter's Ford, * two miles above Chad's ford.

THE BATTLE OF BRANDYWINE, SEPTEMBER II, 1777.

General Kniphausen, commander of the Hessians, came in great force to Chad's ford. At the same time, Lord Cornwallis was making a circuitous march up the Brandywine. He crossed at the Forks and came down upon us rather unexpected. His aim appeared to be to turn our right and, if may be, surround us. The word was soon given to march to the right. We did so,—we moved on to the right four hundred yards. "Face to the front in line with the Maryland troops," was the order, and the battle began.

Cannon balls flew thick and many, from both sides, and small arms roared like the rolling of a drum, for a considerable time, when the word was again given, " March, march to the right! The enemy wants to turn our right." We pushed on to the right and came into an open field. Here we were drawn up and a cannonading began between the British and us. We stood this firing with cannon near an hour, when the word was again given,—" Quick march to the right!"

I was in the centre of our Regiment. We had marched about half-a-mile and crossed a road at right angles when

---

* Query : *Brinton's* Ford ?

Lord Stirling rode up. "Officer," says he, "General Washington is in the rear. Face about!" I did so, as the British were firing on us. I looked about for my Lord, to obey his [*further*] commands, but saw his Lordship whipping and spurring down the road at full gallop!

Some of our soldiers were wounded. I thought, "well, I have no business here fighting in this place. . . . [*I can do no*] good,"—the British aimed to surround [*us* . . .] and with a quick marching, I [*fell back* . . . *and with the*] rest of the Regiment in half-an-hour . . . and about dark and encamped among [. . . *the rest of the army*].

Here follows an anecdote (as nearly as can be deciphered), related to Captain Anderson by some of the soldiers,—who had been eye-witnesses of the incident in the battle,—of a doctor who, he says, remarked he had no business to fight, —("nor had he," the narrator adds),—and who, when the balls flew thickly, ran behind a tree and would then pop his head out and exclaim, "thank God! I am safe yet!" He did this when he came, in succession, near several trees; until finally, thrusting out his head to look back as the army was retreating,—a cannon ball took off his head. "This settled all the Doctor's worldly concerns," adds the writer.

Here then we experienced another drubbing. The times were hard indeed for us poor Yankees. But when it is taken into consideration that our army was not more than one-half the numbers of our enemy, and all things were well appointed and equipped with them, but our army not so,—wanting many things, also having a number of raw recruits,—we did, I think, as well as could be expected.

In fighting this battle of Brandywine, it is thought our great and good Washington made a sacrifice of his own excellent judgment upon the altar of public opinion. Through all these trying times, I saw not a despairing look nor did I hear a despairing word. We had our solacing words always ready for each other,—" Come boys, we shall do better another time,"—sounded throughout our little army. Had any man suggested, merely hinted the idea of giving up,—of relinquishing further opposition,—he would have been knocked down, and if killed it would have been considered as no murder! Such was the spirit of the times, —such were the ideas of us " poor ragamuffins"—(as the British called us)—such were my views, your father's, and thousands of others.

But I am off from my narrative. We marched from Chester to the heights of Darby, seven miles from old Chester, and here our dispersed army made a gathering, to collect its forces. Our army then marched on towards Philadelphia,—came within three miles of the city,—turned to the left,—(keeping on the west bank of the River Schuylkill),—and with a veering to the left and some miles from the river, we encamped at night,—perhaps twenty miles from the battle-ground. Our loss was greater than that of the British, though the loss in our Regiment was small, considering the heavy firing we had come through. It was supposed this was due to the British having shot too high.

I was this night ordered on duty here with one hundred and fifty men,—mostly of the Maryland line,—with three captains, and the suitable number of subalterns. I being the eldest captain, had the command. The German Regiment on our right was commanded by a Prussian baron, a colonel, it was said, in the army of the Great Frederick. An old Prussian major also,—the brigadier-major of the day (Stodart) informed me I must be under the control of the Prussian baron, although he was not commissioned in our army. To this I objected and consulted with the officers of my detachment. They submitted the thing to my decision. I concluded to go with the baron, but to be kept distinct from the German Regiment and not under the control of the baron, but as I saw proper.

After dark we began our march and by daybreak we reached Darby [*Creek*] and a little after sunrise came to old Chester. Here I planted my own sentinels, separate from the Germans. They also did the same, separate from mine. Soon after this was done, the British drums beat about a mile west from us. We were certainly in a dangerous situation,—on the bank of the Delaware,—the enemy close by,—and we were in the land of the Tories. The British were on the march, bearing northwardly. We marched on all this day, keeping near the British army. When they marched,—we marched; when they stopped,—we stopped. Our guide was the beating of their drums. Night came on, there was no house we dare go into ;—we had no tents. I had no blanket even and must make no fire. Some had blankets however. The night was very cold. I kept myself tolerably comfortable by walking about, but was very sleepy and could not sleep for the cold.

The British drums beat by daybreak and we were off

again. A little before sundown, we saw the British in a body coming through a meadow ahead of us. The baron appeared to be very uneasy and we now quick marched towards the Delaware, perhaps ten miles distance. At about twelve o'clock at night we made a short cut to the left, but the next day by sunrise we were again near the British army. We had heavy rains,—were exposed to them all,—were wet to the skin but we walked, say marched, ourselves dry! We continued in this way for several days longer;—near the British through the day,— in the leaves and bushes at night.

On the seventh day from the commencement of the march of the detachment, I learn'd that our army had crossed over to the east bank of the Schuylkill. I inquired for the best ford on the river in that neighborhood as the late rains had raised the waters. We entered the river in platoons,—the river was about two hundred yards wide. I now gave orders to link arm in arm,—to keep close and in a compact form, and to go slow,—keeping their ranks. We moved on,—we found the river breast deep,—it was now night as we gained the western (?) shore all wet, but in safety. We got some fire from a neighboring cottage,—made a fire in the woods,—turned our feet to the fire,—slept comfortably and found our clothes on our backs all dry in the morning.

This day,—I think about the twenty-sixth of September, 1777,—brought us safe to headquarters,—being nine days out;—during which time we never had our clothes off,— lodged in no house,—in a manner on half allowance of provisions and had to beg on the road. Yes, one day I bounced into a house,—hap-at-a-venture,—determined to have something for my stowing-bags. Two handsome young girls met me at the portals of their temple. (We had flour and meat, but did not dare make a fire to cook it, as we were always near the enemy.) I told them my necessity,—that I must have something for my soldiers to eat, and I would pay them for it. They both spoke at once,—as generally females do! "No, no,"—say they both at the same time,—"although you are in the land of Tories, we are no Tories. We have six loaves of bread and plenty of milk and buttermilk." These were immediately given out and our soldiers fared sumptuously.

I was myself very hungry, but said nothing. But I was soon satisfied,—the table was spread directly and I must eat with the two pretty girls, which I did. I ventured to ask them many questions and they told me in reply they had a large and valuable farm belonging to them,—that they had a negro woman,—a man cropped the place through the year; who with the negro woman formed their whole family. They kept a great dairy. Your uncle loved both those girls, but the soldiers must be off and I never saw them more, though I intended it and they desired it. I put it down as one of the errors of my life and charge myself with the black crime of ingratitude.

Now why so prolix, when a gun was not fired on either side? I will tell you. My sufferings on this tour gave myself and all of us an everlasting remembrance. The Germans had much the advantage of us;—they were apprized of the expedition they were going on and therefore prepared to meet it. I was warned, and so was all the rest of our party, to appear on grand parade as a common guard for twenty four hours; and of course was not prepared. The old baron I never saw more,—the Major I did;—he was glad, he said, to see Captain *Anderzun*, as he called me, once more. I thought well of this man.

Now, my good nephew, if this long story does not suit your vocabulary, throw it aside among the chapter of accidents and consign it to the tomb of the Capulets! General Washington gave no further opposition to General Howe, —the roads and passes were left open for him, and he entered the city of Philadelphia without further interruption, where he was received with open arms by the Tories.

Your uncle with affection,

ENOCH ANDERSON.

ALEX^R. ANDERSON, ESQ^R.

May 27, 1819.

1794–1869.

NUMBER SIX.

NUMBER five concluded with the entrance of General Howe into Philadelphia. He advanced his army six miles north of the city, in line from Delaware to Schuylkill, through Germantown. General Washington ordered our army to Perkiomen, about twenty miles from Germantown.

On the third day of October, '77, the lieutenant-colonel of our Regiment—(Pope*)—came to me in the dusk of

---

* Lieutenant-Colonel Charles Pope (1748–1803) was born at Smyrna, Kent County, Delaware, and was a merchant at the commencement of the Revolution. He was probably the son of Thomas Pope of that place. Colonel Pope first served as a captain in Colonel Haslet's, and afterwards as lieutenant-colonel in Colonel Hall's Delaware Regiment till the close of 1779, when he resigned on account of wounds received in service. (See "Minutes of the Council of the Delaware State," December 29, 1779. Papers of Historical Society of Delaware, No. VI. pp. 516, 517, Wilmington, Delaware, 1887.) He was afterwards (1781) appointed by the General Assembly " to the command of the State schooner and barge for the protection of the bay and river of Delaware." (*Ibid.*, November 9, 1781, and January 21, 1783, pp. 668, 669 and 766, 767.) He removed to Georgia prior to 1800, and died and was buried on his farm in Columbia County in that State.

He appears to have been in command of the Delaware regiment at and after the battle of Germantown, as Colonel Hall is reported as wounded in that battle and not rejoining his regiment, owing to disability from wound. Colonel Pope is said to have been a bold and dashing officer. (See History of Delaware State Cincinnati, pp. 68, 69; also Whiteley's " Revolutionary Soldiers of Delaware." (Papers of Historical Society of Delaware, No. XIV. p. 55, Wilmington, Delaware, 1896.)

the evening and told me he was appointed by General Sullivan,—(who commanded the division in which the Delaware Regiment was included, together with the Maryland line and Colonel Hazen's Regiment),—to choose out forty five men,—rank and file,—out of different regiments in the division, to attack the British guards at Mount Airy,* at the entrance of Germantown before day. Each officer and soldier, for fear of confusion in the dark, was ordered to put in their hats a piece of white paper.

"I have chosen you out of our regiment," said Colonel Pope, "pick your officers and men and [*fall*] in on the left of the regiment."

BATTLE OF GERMANTOWN, OCTOBER 4, 1777.

General Washington had got some reinforcements that emboldened him to attack the enemy. Pope called for me at dark—I was ready. "Mind," says he, "when we come to Mount Airy, we are to give one fire and then make a rush with the bayonet." We were called the "forlorn hope." The whole army marched in different divisions and by different roads.

After dark, the entire army moved on to the attack ;—our division, commanded by General Sullivan, in the centre of the army on the Germantown road. We came to Chestnut Hill, three miles from Mount Airy ;—it was then daybreak. Pope came to me and said the object of an attack at Mount Airy was given up,—being too late,—"but keep your

---

* Written incorrectly in the original manuscript Mount *Ring*.

place," said he, " in the line of the regiment, on the left."
The Maryland troops were in our front.

The guard at Mount Airy gave one fire and gave way.
Our division displayed to the right,—on the right of the
Germantown road. We pushed down all fences in our
front and marched to the battle. It was a very foggy
morning. Bullets began to fly on both sides,—some were
killed,—some wounded, but the order was to advance. We
advanced in line of the division,—the firing on both sides
increased,—and what with the thickness of the air and the
firing of guns, we could see but a little way before us.

My position in the line brought me and my party opposite the British infantry behind a small breastwork, and
here began the hardest battle I was ever in,—at thirty feet
distance. Firing from both sides was kept up for some
time, all in darkness. My men were falling very fast. I
now took off my hat and shouted as loud as I could,—
" Charge bayonets and advance !" They did so, to a man,
—(the roar of cannon and small arms was great at this
time);—the British heard me and run for it. I lost four
men killed on this spot, and about twenty wounded.

We proceeded on into the heart of Germantown and
soon were in possession of a part of their artillery,—about
thirty pieces,—and among their tents. But the tables were
soon turned. Both our wings had given way,—the British
brought their force to the centre,—and of course we had to
retreat, but our regiment came off in good order. Let it be
observed here,—once for all ;—*the Delaware Regiment was
never broken,—no, not in the hottest fire.*

We got to the Perkiomen again at night. Here, we old

soldiers had marched forty miles,—fought a battle to three o'clock, P.M.—and marched back to camp again. We eat nothing and drank nothing but water, on the tour!

BIOGRAPHY OF CAPTAIN HOLLAND.

Captain Holland had resigned the duties of an adjutant and became a captain in the line of the regiment. He was mortally wounded at the battle of Germantown and was brought on two miles in advance of White Marsh. I retreated on the Schuylkill road, where Pope and I had a conversation on the situation of Holland. It was agreed between us that I should go the next day on Colonel Pope's horse, to give our friend Holland what aid and comfort we could. When I mounted the Colonel's horse to go upon this errand, I felt awkward indeed,—not having been on the back of a horse for nearly two years past. It was twelve o'clock before I started.

In the evening, I saw Holland,—he was lying in ruins. The women of the house had known me from infancy. I had been brought up in the neighborhood, until I was fourteen years of age. "Why, Sophia," says I,—(she was a Quaker),—"do you know me?" "Yes, I know thee bravely," she replied. "Well," said I, "I have no time now to talk about old times, but have you not got a wounded officer in your house?" "Yes I have," said she, "and the British officers called in here and told me he was a worthy man,—that he had been a captain in their service, and to take good care of him."

Holland then told me there was nothing in the house fitted to his condition. I asked Sophia where the suitable things could be had. She told me, at White Marsh, at Mr. West's;—"but thee will be in great danger," she added, "if thee goes, for the British Light Horse were at White Marsh about two hours ago." But notwithstanding her warning, I ventured. Mr. West gave me two bottles of wine, some tea and loaf sugar; for all which he would receive nothing. When I got back it was dark. I took a long and affectionate farewell of my old friend. I never saw him more.

I set my face towards camp,—there was no abiding place here for me with safety. I rode on towards headquarters. I stopped at a house off the road,—the man and his wife had known me from infancy. They were very kind to me, but under apprehension of the British taking me prisoner. "For," said they, "the British dragoons go several times every day up the road above this, and back again." I stayed here this night, however, and was off by daylight in the morning,—got safe to our camp and gave an account of myself and my doings.

The British about this time drew in their army near the city and a resolution was formed by our officers to bring Holland to our camp. I was out of camp a few days, as I went to Bethlehem, thirty miles north of Perkiomen for some clothes. (Our baggage had been sent there previous to the battle of Germantown.) On my returning, I found Holland had been brought up and well lodged in a house, in the neighborhood of the camp, where he could have the best medical aid and a proper attention paid him. But alas! the wound was mortal,—he died.

He was indeed one of the children of misfortune,—born

under a fiery planet. Like your old uncle, never to be worth
a groat in his life and [*to suffer*] other harms.

In May, '76, Holland told me the following story, as
near as I can recollect. That he entered the British army
in early youth,—that he was at the battles of Dettingen and
Fontenoy, in Germany,—that by his merits he was taken
notice of and appointed a captain in Colonel—or, say Lord
—Montague's regiment. He now got married and lived
in London. He was sent with his company and stationed
at a town some miles distant from London. Here he became acquainted with the parson of the parish. The parson had a handsome daughter,—well accomplished and
very interesting, and he had real friendship for the parson
and his daughter. Holland was called to London, and
some time after he heard that this modest virgin had given
way to the arts of seduction and was now in London. He
was shocked,—he searched, but could not find her,—but she
heard where he was and sent for him. He came, and found
her on the bed of death.

" Captain Holland," said she, " you are the only friend I
have on earth. For my wrong doings my father has cast
me off, and now I am going to lay you under the strongest
injunctions." " Anything I can do, Miss," [*replied Holland*],
" shall be done for you." " The obligation I wish to lay
you under," said she, " is to do an act of justice. Two
young noblemen, with whom I have been acquainted, re-
cently outrageously maltreated me. I hesitated at the time
to mention it to the people of the house and now I find
myself dying. The whole family of this house are witness
[*of the truth of this*], from the outcry I made at the time."

Holland promised,—soon after the lady died, and he brought suit against the two young noblemen; but with false witnesses, false swearing, &c., they were cleared.

Now the colonel of the regiment he belonged to,—(Montague),—was uncle to these two young noblemen. He sent for Holland. "Well, Captain Holland," said he, "you have done your [*best*] endeavour to ruin my nephews;—now you shall be tried by a court-martial or resign." "Let me sell my commission," said Holland, "I can get a thousand guineas for it." "You shall not," said the Colonel. Holland knew the power of the great,—knew he had no chance for justice. "Here then," said he, "is my commission,"— and gave it to the colonel. "I now," said Holland to him, "go to the land of liberty, where a poor man is something in the scale of being."

Holland had two sons,—one about six, the other about four years old,—left with a friend in London. He went to this friend and told him his situation. "I will be a father unto your two sons," said his friend,—"I will have them educated and put to trades [*afterwards*]." Holland embraced his friend and his children;—it was their last embrace,—he never saw them more. He came to Philadelphia in the year '75;—you know the rest.*

Captain Holland was a handsome man,—portly,—well

---

* Captain Holland was an officer in the Pennsylvania establishment before being commissioned in the Delaware regiment. He appears on the roster of officers of the Fourth Pennsylvania Battalion (Colonel Anthony Wayne, commanding), as being commissioned second lieutenant January 8, 1776, appointed adjutant January 11, and resigning on March 15, in the same year. (See Pennsylvania State Archives, 2d series, vol. x. p. 120.)

formed,—had all the appearance of a soldier, and was a soldier indeed. I have been prolix on this matter,—a biographical sketch of my old friend. Captain Holland (I think), had been a widower * some time previous to his leaving England. He came poor to this country, and died so.

Your affectionate uncle,

ENOCH ANDERSON.

ALEX^R. ANDERSON, ESQ^R.
   May 29, 1819.

---

* This is probably an error. The General Assembly of Delaware in 1781 passed a resolution, in response to " a petition of Joanna Holland, *widow of Captain Thomas Holland*, of the Delaware Regiment, who was slain in the service of the United States at the battle of Germantown in October, 1777," for the payment of forty pounds to said Joanna Holland, etc. (See " Minutes of the Council of the Delaware State," November 10, 1781. Papers Historical Society of Delaware, No. VI. pp. 672, 673.) *Mrs. Joanna Holland's* name also appears at foot of pay-roll of officers of Delaware Regiment for payment of said amount. It would have been impossible for such payment to have been made to a person not so entitled, with the cognizance of twenty-one officers, all of whom had known and served with her husband, and who united in the presentation of the petition of the widow of Captain Holland to the General Assembly of the State. (See *Ibid.*, p. 681.)

NUMBER SEVEN.

My number six concluded with the funeral of my friend Holland. About this time came the glorious news of the surrender of Burgoyne. A day of jubilee indeed, and a day of rejoicing throughout our army,—as well as to all the well wishers of their country, and to this land of Liberty!

OF CORPORAL TRAYSON.

I had a corporal in my company, called Manuel Trayson, —a German by birth,—about thirty-six years of age,— active, sprightly,—a sort of soldier of fortune. He had been in the German service,—also in the Spanish and Portu- guese service. He spoke, in his broken English, more like a Frenchman than a German. Some old soldiers in Europe, —(perhaps in this country too),—have got a conception that by some cant words or prayer, they can ward off all bullets in battle.

Some days antecedent to the battle of Germantown, Manuel come to me,—(I was in my tent alone),—and said to me: "Vell Ca-pe-a-teen, I does vant to spake vid you." "Sit down, Manuel," says I. "If you vil gif me de von quart visky, I dell you a barticular brayer;—shall touch you not von bullet in all battles." "Manuel," I replied, "a can- teen of whisky stands by the tent-pole,—take a joram." He did so. "But suppose I want confidence and faith in

113957

this prayer?"   "Den I pe sorree,—vairy sorree, sar;—for mitout de fait, it too you no cood."

Manuel went away.   Much grape-shot was fired from Chew's House in Germantown on the day of the battle. Manuel was a gallant fellow and behaved well in the battle. A grape-shot had gone through the face of his cocked hat, —of which he was not a little proud.

A few days after the battle, I spoke to him.   "Well, Manuel," says I, "what do you think of that particular prayer you wanted to learn me before the battle?"   Manuel stamped with his right foot three or four times on the ground.   "I vil tell you, Ca-pe-a-teen, vat I tink ov dem dings;—de brayer pees vairy coot and strong vor de small pullets,—*put var tem tam crape-shot; I don't know vat do dink!*"

Reinforcements came and our army marched nearer to the enemy, on the Skippack Road near White Marsh;—and not long after, our army encamped here at White Marsh, on all the commanding eminences.   This was about the beginning of December, '77.   Your father was here then,—I saw him frequently.   This was the place of his birth, as I before told you.

OF CAPTAIN POLLOCK.

I had been acquainted with this man in Sussex [*County*], Delaware.   He was captain of a company of militia light-horse;—a bold, daring, enterprising man,—a warm Whig,— a warm friend to his country.

He came into my tent one day,—pale and wan,—and told me the following story.   That the Tories in Sussex had surrounded his house in the night,—took him prisoner,—

bound him,—put him on board of a vessel in the Bay, and sent him to Philadelphia to General Howe. Howe ordered him to the dungeon of the New Prison. Here were about thirty prisoners in all, in this horrid hole. He was determined not to stay here,—he roused his fellow-prisoners,— (he had friends in the city),—he got tools,—they dug out. It was moonlight. He was the foremost man,—he had a small crow-bar in his hands. He knocked down the sentinel, run for the Schuylkill,—there was no ice in the river, —he swam it and came to me. What became of his comrades in misery, he knew not,—every one was to shift for himself.

The weather getting cold, General Washington built huts at Valley Forge,—sixteen miles or more from Philadelphia —and sent General Smallwood of the Maryland line with the Maryland troops, the Delaware Regiment and Hazen's Regiment to Wilmington, (Delaware), twenty-eight miles below Philadelphia, and near the Delaware. Our division so called, did not exceed fifteen hundred men, but report made it double that number.

Here then we were stationed for the winter, twenty-eight miles from headquarters. Comparing our numbers with the British, our situation was critical and dangerous; but the idea of numbers,—*i.e.*, of the militia at our backs,—no doubt had its due effect.

The British being straitened for provisions, sent down the river flat-bottomed boats and had carried much off already. General Smallwood sent for me about ten o'clock one night,—(about the first of January, 1778);—it was sleeting and raining, and a dark night. " Here," said the

General, "you must go on detachment at once. Here are one hundred and fifty men, with suitable officers, &c. Take the command of the party, explore the shores of the Delaware down to Hamburg, and [*do*] as you see proper;—for this night the enemy will be down the river. I shall send fifteen or twenty wagons after you; load them all from the rich farms on the Delaware,—leaving enough however for their home consumption,—and give written orders on me for payment."

We set off and got to Hamburg. By daylight, the wagons came. I had them all loaded and sent them on to the garrison. But one boat appeared from Philadelphia. We hailed him,—he would not come to, until he was fired on and one man wounded. I marched for Wilmington with the six prisoners I had taken in the boat; being gone seven days.

I was frequently sent by General Smallwood on such partizan matters;—he hearing I had been brought up in the neighborhood. One time, (in February), I had one hundred and twenty men with me. I went to Hamburg and lower down the Delaware. Early one morning a lieutenant of my party asked me what we should do; there being no enemy here. "Look about you," said I, "the soldier's eye should be ever vigilant. See that man-of-war, not more than a mile from here and near our shore." He took the hint and asked me to let him have thirty men. "Yes," I said, "and in welcome." He came back in the evening with eight prisoners, and gave me the following account.

"I went," said he, "to a farmer's house and exchanged my regimentals for a farmer's suit of clothes. I then went and placed myself [*with my men*], under the marsh bank opposite to the man-of-war. I got upon the bank and halloed that I had cheese, lamb, mutton and other good things. A boat was immediately sent with about a dozen men. When they landed, the boatswain called for me to come down and bring my things. I told him I was not able, that they must come to me. They ran up—'Where are your goods?' says the boatswain. 'Here,' says the farmer, pointing his finger to his men under the bank, ready to fire. Eight gave up,—the others got among the reeds. The ship then 'began firing,—observing the confusion and noise on the shore,—but" [*said the lieutenant*], "I and my party all got safely in." I was on many such parties through the winter.

THE WOOD-FLAT.

Colonel Pope—(our lieutenant-colonel, and who had been a sea-captain)—came to me in March, '78. "I have been looking for you, Captain," said he. "See yonder there lays at anchor, at the creek's mouth, the Falmouth packet and a sloop. They have nothing but wooden guns. Get you thirty or forty men and I will get a piece of artillery. There is a wood-flat at the wharf for us." I got my men, —he got his piece of cannon, and away we went, down the creek. Pope was captain of our little man-of-war,—(the "Wood-Flat"),—I was captain of marines!

As we drew near to the enemy, they gave us a broadside, but of small calibre. "Pope," says I, "where are their *wooden* guns?" (Besides they had netting ten feet from the water's edge.) "No chance for us," said Pope. I did not think so either, but we concluded to fight and the battle began at two o'clock, P.M.

We fired our piece of artillery until all the quarter-rails of our wood-flat were torn off;—the enemy slipped their cables and fell down the river. Whether we done them any injury or not, I know not. We received no harm, save from one bullet that struck us. "A bloodless battle," say you.

We got safe to Wilmington at dusk and I walked six miles the same evening, to a ball at New Castle.

Your affectionate uncle,

ENOCH ANDERSON.

ALEX^R. ANDERSON, ESQ^R.

   June 9, 1819.

NUMBER EIGHT.

NUMBER seven ended with the expedition on the Wood-Flat and a sort of drawn battle, on the Delaware,—and a ball afterwards. This latter was about commencing as I entered. Captain Rice—(your father knew him well)—told me they wanted the proper spirit for the occasion,—being under alarm on account of the firing up the river. All were gloomy and sad, but I soon set them at ease by a short explanation of the cause. All hearts then sprung to joy usual on the spur of such occasions, and we all passed a pleasing and cheerful evening.

Next morning, by ten o'clock, I was at Wilmington and waited upon our general at headquarters, who wanted to see me. "Well, young man," said he, "I want you to go on detachment, but I fear between fighting all yesterday and dancing all night, you are too much fatigued to scout."

"I don't feel so, general," I replied, "I never felt so [*well*] in my life."

"Well then go," said he, "there are a hundred and fifty men—take the command of them."

I went accordingly,—was gone eight days,—had no adventures worth relating,—returned and made my report to the general. He was satisfied and paid me some compliments. "Anderson," said he, "you are what is called a jolly,—a merry fellow,—a little wild and love dancing,—but I find you punctual and faithful to your duties."

I loved this old General Smallwood,—he was a worthy man and a good soldier,—a man of excellent understanding. After the war, he was Governor of Maryland. He is dead long since.

It was now May, '78. I had frequently gone to New Castle to see my mother and my little brothers and sisters, and when the coast was clear,—*i.e.*, none of the British men-of-war in the river,—to stay there all night. On one of these visits a Tory called me [*to*] one side, telling me he wanted to speak to me privately. "You know what I am," said he, "and I know what you are. Well, I have respect for you and all your family,—therefore, for God's sake, sleep no more at your mother's house. Two hundred guineas are offered for you, dead or alive. They will surround you in the night at your mother's—bind you, and send you on to Philadelphia, a prisoner."

I asked him the reason of all this. "Why, because you have cut off all their resources of provisions along the Delaware, and have taken their men prisoners." "I thank you, —heartily thank you,"—I replied, and left him. After this warning, I slept no more at my mother's house.

OF ADJUTANT LUCAS.

After Captain Holland took post as captain in the line of the Regiment, Lucas was appointed our adjutant.* He

---

* John Lucas appears as adjutant on the "roll of Field, Staff and Company Officers of the Delaware Regiment of Foot, on the Continental establishment, commanded by Colonel David Hall, on the arrangement of April 5, 1777." This roll, which is in the handwriting of Ensign Caleb P. Bennett, is now in the possession of the Delaware State Society of the Cincinnati. (See History

made a good one, but nothing equal to Holland. He was about thirty-six years of age,—full of life and motion. He had belonged to the Welsh Fusilleers and had deserted. After staying some time with our Regiment, he resigned,— went as captain of marines in a privateer from Philadelphia, —was taken,—discovered,—known, and hung at the yard-arm in the harbour of New York. An end to poor Lucas! A man I thought well of.

Our division was now commanded to march and ordered to Valley Forge,—General Washington's headquarters, where we arrived all in due order. I took a furlough and went to the State of Delaware on my own private business. Before my return to camp, the British had evacuated Philadelphia and the battle of Monmouth was fought. (Your father was in this battle.) The army was now marched to White Plains. This was a barren campaign in the Middle States.

The British had now turned their attention [*to the towns*] along the defenceless shores of Connecticut and to the southward. All their steps were marked with blood and plunder.

All the rest of my time in the army would be quite un-interesting to you,—such as marching and countermarch-ing, scouting-parties, guards, &c.,—all bloodless and wound-less. I here then draw to a close this little sketch of my history;—make, my good boy, what you please of it,—it is

---

of Delaware Cincinnati, p. 75.) Lieutenant George Purvis, being reported as adjutant of the Regiment in 1778–1780 (see *ibid.* p. 78), is accounted for by the fate of Adjutant Lucas as above stated.

for your use. My youngest son, Lucius,* takes copies of all I write, as an archive for the family and that all my children may see on record the sufferings of their father in the morning of his days and [*to learn like him*] how to rough the storms of life and those of war. I am now able to look upwards and thank my God that throughout all these trying scenes, I was not one day sick.

In the year 1779, I told our field-officers I would resign. To this, however, they would not hear, but said I should have a nine months' or a year's furlough. I left the camp soon after.

My brother Inslee was in the battle of Brandywine and Germantown. He was a cadet in Colonel Proctor's Regiment of Artillery. After he left the army, I got him a commission of adjutant in Colonel Gibson's Regiment. He was killed at General St. Clair's defeat.†

Of your father's history in the war, I know no more than what I have told you,—being distant and separate from him most of the time. As near as I can remember, I was in thirteen battles,—great and small;—once a stout, active

---

* Enoch Lucius Anderson was born January 25, 1797, in Cumberland County, Penna., and died April 9, 1871, at Titusville, Crawford County, Penna. He was an elder of the Presbyterian church and a prominent member of the community in which he lived.

† Inslee Anderson was adjutant in Colonel Gibson's regiment at the time of his death in St. Clair's defeat by the Indians of the Northwest Territory, November 4, 1791, and was so reported with Captain Robert Kirkwood (killed in the same battle), in the official letter from General St. Clair to General Knox, Secretary of War, dated Fort Washington, November 9, 1791, and transmitted by President Washington to Congress, December 12, 1791. (See "Delaware Gazette" (Wilmington, Del.), December 17, 1791.)

man,—now am an old, lame cripple ;—in a manner good for nothing. Write me [*in reply*] on these matters,—farewell and may the Lord have you in His holy keeping. All our loves and good wishes go herewith from us all, to you all.

Your old uncle, with a warm affection,

ENOCH ANDERSON.

ALEXANDER ANDERSON, ESQ^R.

June 15, 1819.